NEW MEXICO, U.S.A.

A PHOTOGRAPHIC ESSAY OF NEW MEXICO

CREATED AND EDITED BY BARBARA ERDMAN
DESIGNED BY MARY SHAPIRO

Published by The Santa Fe Center for Photography   Santa Fe, New Mexico

Designed by Mary Shapiro

Typeset by Casa Sin Nombre, Santa Fe

Color Separations, Duotones and Halftones by Chroma-Graphics, Inc., Kansas City, Missouri

Printed by The Lowell Press, Kansas City, Missouri

Bound by Universal Book Bindery Services Inc., San Antonio, Texas

Santa Fe Center for Photography
104 West San Francisco Street
Santa Fe, New Mexico 87501

Printed in the United States of America

ISBN 0-9615298-0-6 H
ISBN 0-9615298-1-4 S

I am indebted to Cissie Ludlow and Murrae Haynes for all their help and supportiveness. Without Cissie, especially, this project would never have succeeded. I would also like to thank Marcella Fabbri, who started it all.

My appreciation and gratitude go to Paul Caponigro for being the first photographer to accept, Paul Logsdon and David Noble for help and advice, and Barbara Van Cleve for finding us our printer. My gratitude also goes to Herb Lotz for donating his time and skill preparing transparencies for this book, Jonathan Morse for legal advice, to Casa Sin Nombre for the typography and the New Mexico State archives for help with the history, and finally to Payson Lowell and the Lowell Press of Kansas City, for all the care and concern they have shown.

I would also like to thank for their generosity in helping this project become more than a dream:
Sunwest Bank
Roy Berlin

Murrae Haynes "Welcome Home" Front Cover

HISTORY

This history was based on "A Brief History of the State of New Mexico," by Dr. Stanley M. Hordes, State Historian and Dr. Donald R. Lavash, Historian, New Mexico Records Center and Archives; and Regge Wiseman, Museum of New Mexico, contained in the OFFICIAL NEW MEXICO BLUE BOOK, 1981-82.

New Mexico is the fifth largest state in the Union. It is larger than Italy. The terrain varies from deserts and barren plains to piney forests, from 2,817 feet (845 m.) at the town of Red Bluff to Wheeler Peak at 13,161 feet (3948 meters) above sea level. Most of the population lives at 5000 feet above sea level or higher.

People think of New Mexican history as beginning with the arrival of the Spanish. In fact, it has been dated back 12,000 years to Clovis Culture. These prehistoric people and their descendants were largely nomadic hunters who lived on now extinct mammoths, bison, and early forms of camels and horses. With the retreat of the glaciers, the terrain began drying up, the types of vegetation changed and the herds moved. Man became more dependent upon plants and only supplemented his diet by hunting. This lifestyle continued until about the time of Christ.

At this time corn was introduced from Mexico, and the people in the western two-thirds of the state began farming and developing permanent and semi-permanent villages with a more substantial architecture and a little later, pottery. During this time the people in the eastern third of the state retained their semi-nomadic lifestyle, which continued for the next several centuries.

After 500 A.D., the more western communities became more condensed, and regional differences in architecture and pottery emerged. They began building pueblo style houses and special ceremonial buildings (kivas). Society became more complicated. Between 1100 and 1400 A.D. vast areas of New Mexico were abandoned possibly because of climate changes, though some areas remained in use as evidenced by the Spanish.

The first Europeans entered New Mexico in 1540, led by Francisco Vásquez de Coronado. While they did not find the wealth and precious metals they were seeking, they did find groups of advanced sedentary Indians who they called "Pueblos" because they lived in towns. They returned to Mexico, and fifty years later, in 1598, the Spanish returned for more permanent colonization, when Juan de Oñate was appointed governor of New Mexico and was directed by the viceroy of New Spain to settle the area along the upper Río Grande. Accompanied by some 200 settlers, including soldiers, families and priests, and over 7000 head of livestock, Oñate headed north along the Camino Real. He established his headquarters first at San Juan, and just months later at San Gabriel. In 1610 the capital was established at the Villa de Santa Fe, making Santa Fe the oldest capital city in what is now the United States.

Albuquerque, now the largest city in New Mexico (population 342,000) was first settled in 1706.

New Mexico in the seventeenth century was plagued by isolation, conflicts between civil and ecclesiastical authorities, and extreme demands placed by the Spanish settlers on the native population. The last situation became so bad that by 1680 the Pueblo Indians revolted and successfully drove out the Spanish. Thirteen years later the Spanish, under the direction of Diego de Vargas recaptured New Mexico. In an attempt to encourage settlement the Spanish issued land grants for agriculture and grazing to Spanish colonists and reconfirmed the property rights of the Pueblos.

In the seventeenth century the Spanish had emphasized the Christianization of the Indians through the Franciscans. After the reconquest the emphasis switched to military defense. The Spanish were concerned with the expansion of the French and attacks by the Plains Indians. This resulted in the formation of the Provincias Internas, a jurisdictional unit that was formed of Texas, New Mexico, Arizona, California and part of northern Mexico. Gradually during the late eighteenth and early nineteenth centuries concern for the French was replaced by concern for the English and the new Anglo-Americans.

With the independence of Mexico from Spain in 1821, the Spanish policy of protectionism was abandoned in favor of open trade, the Santa Fe Trail was born and with it, increased exploitation of New Mexican markets. It became more difficult for the new Mexican government to administrate its northern provinces, including New Mexico. The secession of Texas from Mexico and its subsequent annexation by the United States strained relations. The United States developed a feeling that it was its "manifest destiny" to possess the entire North American continent. In May, 1846, Americans invaded Mexico and began the Mexican War. Three months later, U.S. Army troops marched unopposed across northern New Mexico into Santa Fe. In 1848 by the Treaty of Guadalupe Hidalgo, the United States paid Mexico fifteen million dollars for New Mexico, Arizona and California, and under the terms of the Compromise of 1850, New Mexico was granted status as a Territory of the United States.

At this time gold was discovered in California and as a result of the great migrations there, people began also settling in New Mexico. The Santa Fe Trail was the most important supply route connecting the east with the west.

During the Civil War, New Mexico was with the North. The Confederates captured it, but held it for only two weeks before being forced to retreat to Texas.

Problems in the interpretation of Spanish and Mexican land laws in the late nineteenth century worked to the disadvantage of Hispanic landholders as well as Indian Pueblos. Poorly defined boundaries and the lack of original documentation led the U.S. Office of the Surveyor General to dismiss many claims. New arrivals from the east and shrewd attorneys took advantage of the situation by acquiring the valuable lands now made available to them. Finally in 1891 a Court of Private Land Claims was established to review the situation. It also proved inadequate. Today there are still cases being heard in the courts to settle disputes that go back to the original land grants.

New Mexico was admitted to the Union as the 47th State in 1912. At that time it was mainly agricultural with a growing mining industry. Later oil was discovered, and with the growing use of automobiles, tourism became an important industry. World War II saw the development of military bases and today New Mexico, for better or worse, is one of the largest centers for nuclear research. Los Alamos was created to coordinate the Manhattan Project which resulted in the development of the first atomic bomb, which was detonated at White Sands, near Alamogordo. Later Sandia National Laboratories was established in Albuquerque to develop weapons for military use. The Los Alamos Laboratories are now working on peaceful as well as military uses of nuclear energy, and also on the Laser Weapons Technology. An experimental Nuclear Waste Isolation Pilot Project is being set up at Carlsbad to bury nuclear wastes.

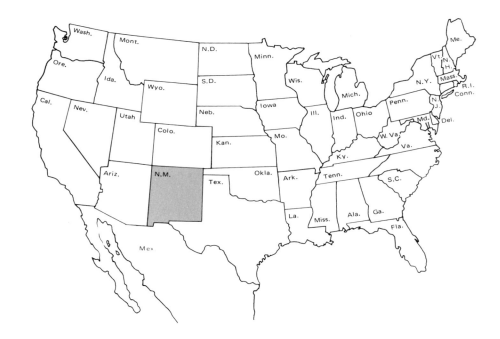

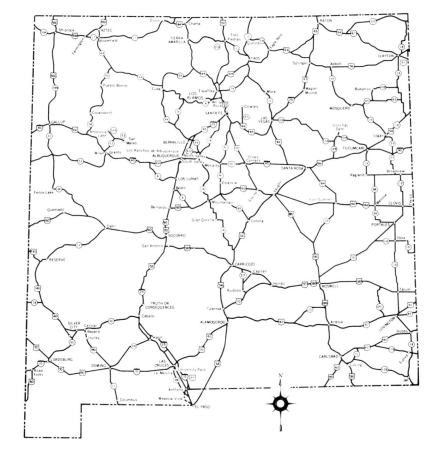

INTRODUCTION

Barbara Erdman   *Santo Niño, Santuario de Chimayo*

Imagine yourself in a wagon train traveling with no real roads over a difficult terrain with little water. In some places the vegetation is so sparse that it takes 11 acres for one cow to graze. The sun is scorching through your clothes. You see storm clouds gathering on the horizon. Lightning is flashing. It hits a tree nearby. All of sudden the dried up dirt at your feet becomes a torrential river. Ten minutes later the water is gone and along with it went a great deal of debris and some of your things. The altitude puts you out of breath. And there is the ever present fear of those strange people whose land you are taking or traveling through. Every day of survival must be like an exhausted miracle. What incredible courage, tenacity and desperation the original pioneers must have had to come out here. On my first visit to New Mexico I was overwhelmed with this awareness. Coming from large cities both in the United States and in Europe it was a new consciousness for me. The weather wasn't something to ignore if possible and to be gotten through, it was something to participate in. For the first time I could understand those tales of people going out into the desert to commune with nature who were never seen again. Here you are confronted with raw untamable forces. It makes one small, but it also makes one very grand indeed. The magnificence is hard to conceptualize. The awesomeness brings you very close to God or the Cosmos, or whatever you wish to call it.

This spirituality has made New Mexico a magnet for various groups, religious and esoteric. While historically the Catholics have predominated, the Penitente live in communities round about the northern part of the state. There is a healing shrine at Chimayo, where dirt from the Chimayo River is rubbed on the ailing, and many cures have been truly performed. The Muslim have built a mosque at Abiquiu, the Sikh's have a major ashram at Española. Mormons are here as are all the Christian faiths and the Jews. And there seems with all this variety to be a tremendous amount of tolerance—or I should say a fierce individualism— "you let me do my thing and you can do yours."

Perhaps all this is possible because of the basic tri-cultural nature of the place. In New Mexico the divisions culturally are Native American (Indian), Hispanic and all the rest (Anglo). While frictions exist amongst these groups there is a stronger sense of acceptance.

Politically it is a state made up of enclaves or pockets of beliefs. Many people assume that New Mexico is very conservative. Actually it is not. While the southern part of the state has areas that are reactionary, and Albuquerque is moderately conservative, large areas are quite liberal, especially Santa Fe and the Northern part of the state. New Mexico was one of the first states to pass the Equal Rights Amendment. It is a state now in the forefront fighting child abuse. In spite of it being a playground for the rich, especially around the ski and resort areas, the average income is just a little over $10,000 a year. There is a tremendous amount of poverty, but you don't find slums as in other parts of the United States. There is a cultural tradition here that mitigates the situation—the barter system, and also a strong family tradition of looking after one's own.

The fragility of life is a constant awareness; partly because of the raw and difficult aspects of living here, partly because of the nuclear research being done here, and partly because of being a prime target area in case of war. New Mexicans accept adversity and are nurtured by the grandeur of nature. People here thrive on the continual challenge and demand for self-sufficiency. It is also one of the few places left where there is so much of a sense of aloneness and space, that the emptiness of the place is filling. People love New Mexico or they leave it. But for those who stay the magic is undeniable.

Imagine yourself at night wandering in a piñon forest near Tierra Amarilla feeling the closeness of the stars and you meet the shadowy form of a woman crying for her lost children. She is La Llorona, a local ghost. Will you help her find her children? Or perhaps some night at Chimayo you will come across the effigy of the Santo Niño doing some good deeds and getting his shoes dirty. Will you leave a new pair for him at the Santuario? Or perhaps some day you may be driving along Route 385 and you see a flying saucer. . . . .

Welcome to New Mexico, the Land of Enchantment.

Barbara Erdman

Santa Fe, 1985

Ike Fordyce *Tent Rocks*

David Noble *Pueblo Blanco*

10

David Noble *Pueblo Bonito, Chaco Canyon*

William Davis *"Mythic Fortress", Taos*

Jack Parsons *Monticello*

Lisa Law *Romolo, The Goat Herder, Truchas*

Miradel Rubenstein *Silvanita Lopez, Cordova, N.M.*

Roswell Angier *Lake Valley, (Navajo Reservation)*

James Ruffner *"Untitled, 1982"*

James Ruffner *"Untitled, 1982", Albuquerque park*

David Scheinbaum *"Cross of the Martyrs, 1979"* Santa Fe

James Hart *Construction Workers, Santa Fe (Left)*

Janet Russek *Wall Painting, Santa Fe (Below)*

Kevin Bubriski *San Gabriel Cholos*

James Hart *Michael Jackson Poster, Santa Fe Fiesta Parade*

Kevin Bubriski *San Juan Feast Day*

Kevin Bubriski *Guadalupe Feast Day*

Richard Erdoes *Navajo Carnival*

David Noble *Deer Dance, San Juan Pueblo*

Richard Erdoes *Cloud Dance, San Juan Pueblo*

Richard Erdoes *Goat Skinning on a Navajo Reservation*

Susan Zwinger *Chili Ristras*

Deede Phillips   *"Adventures of Lyle Swan", movie set south of Santa Fe*

Judy Moore *Low Riders*

Carm Little Turtle   *"Indian Shotgun" hand colored sepia toned print*

Richard Wickstrom   *Downtown, Akela Flats*

Barbara Van Cleve *Rainstorm in the Desert*

Barbara Simpson *B-52 Bomber hand colored silver print*

Richard Erdoes *Buffalo Dancer, Puje Ceremonial (Right)*

Paul Logsdon *Navajo Sheep in the Checkerboard area*

Paul Logsdon *Plowing in the Mesilla Valley*

Paul Logsdon *Navajo Coal Mine and the Four Corners Power Plant*

Steven Northup *Making Adobe Bricks*

Steven Northup *Taos Pueblo* (Right)

Barbara Erdman *Gormley Lane, Santa Fe* (Far Right)

Edward Klamm *The Gold Bar, Santa Fe*

Roswell Angier   *Gallup Indian Community Center, 1979*
            (Above)

Jeannette Williams   *Rio Grande Zoo, Albuquerque (Right)*

Nancy Hunter Warren *Penitente 2*

Charles Venrick *Our Lady of Guadalupe Procession,*
Santa Fe

Barbara Gluck *Veterans' Day, National Cemetery, November, 1983 (Above)*

Alex Traube *Parade, Las Vegas (Above right)*

Murrae Haynes *Jesse Jackson Rally, The Plaza, Santa Fe (Right)*

James Hart   *Political Rally, Santa Fe*

Edward Klamm *Lota' Burger*

Barbaraellen Koch *Laundromat*

Barbara Erdman   *Central Avenue, Albuquerque*

Roswell Angier   *Gallup City Jail (Right)*

Barbaraellen Koch *State Penitentiary Prison Riot, 1980 (Above)*

Robert Klintworth *Penitentiary of New Mexico (Right)*

44

Stephen Cooper *Downtown Albuquerque*

Bradner Crawford Jones *Oil Rig, northeast of Cerrillos*

Lisa Law *"The Rape of Black Mesa"*

Lisa Law *Power Plant, Four Corners*

Bradner Crawford Jones *Radio Telescope Antenna Field, Datil (Above)*

47

Douglas Kahn *Santa Fe Station (Above)*

Stephen Cooper *Santa Fe Station (Left)*

David Scheinbaum *Bisti Badlands*

Walter Chappell *Monastery Road, Chama River,*
Chama Valley

Willard Van Dyke *White Cliffs, Abiquiu*

William Davis *"Venus and Mars", Rio Grande Gorge, Taos*

Paul Caponigro *"Near Dixon"*

53

Mary Peck *Wagon Mound (Above)*

Robert Saltzman *Quemado (Left)*

James Ruffner *"Untitled, 1982", Albuquerque Backyards*
(Above)

Jeannette Williams *Sheep Herders in Tomá*

Mary Peck *Abbott (Above)*

Richard Wickstrom *"Suburban Rock Garden", Las Cruces*
(Left)

Douglas Kahn *Madrid*

Bernard Plossu *Taos Truck*

Bernard Plossu *Route 666, Between Gallup and Shiprock*

Jack Parsons *On the Pankey Ranch north of Truth or Consequences (Both)*

J.D. Lincoln *Sunday Afternoon, Taos*

62

Barbara Van Cleve *Roundup (Above)*

Barbara Van Cleve *Rodeo (Right)*

Alex Traube   *Downtown, Las Vegas (Left)*

Roswell Angier   *Gallup, 1979 (Far Left)*

Don Greiser   *Albuquerque, hand wound overlapping
exposures (Below)*

Jeannette Williams   *Kress Building, Albuquerque*

Barbaraellen Koch   *Meals on Wheels (A State program for feeding the poor elderly and handicapped in their homes)*

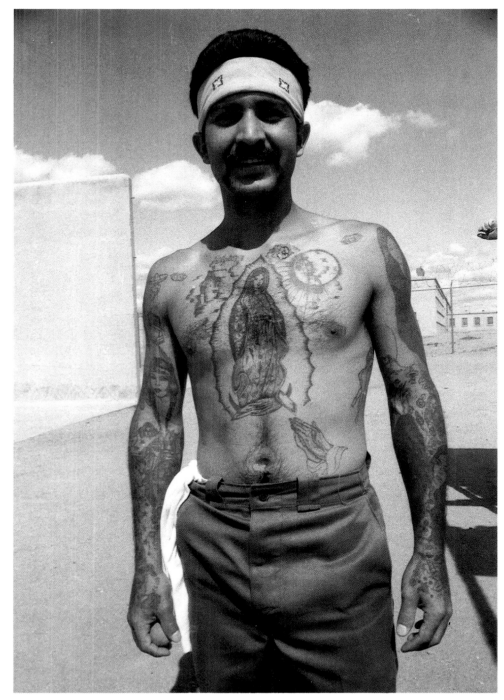 

Barbara Gluck   *Inmate with Tattoos, Front and Back*
Penitentiary of N.M., 1983

Alex Traube *Prom portrait, Las Vegas High School*

68

Nancy Hunter Warren *Morada Alter (Left)*

Kevin Bubriski *Chimayo Wedding (Below)*

Cissy Ludlow *Break Dancers*

Cissie Ludlow *Zozobra*

Cissie Ludlow *Trashchic Fashion Show*

John Whately *Carlsbad Caverns (Above)*

Deede Phillips *Mosque at Abiquiu (Right)*

Orlando Diaz *Church, Jemez Pueblo*

Jack Parsons *Blue Car, Carlsbad*

Rahoul Contractor *Bernalillo County (Above)*

Michael Fahy *Bosque del Apache Wildlife Refuge (Left)*

Charles Venrick *Roswell (hand colored silverprint) (Above)*

Charles Venrick *Two Chairs, Roswell (hand colored silverprint) (Left)*

Barbara Simpson *Beauty Salon, De Vargas Hotel, Santa Fe (Far Left)*

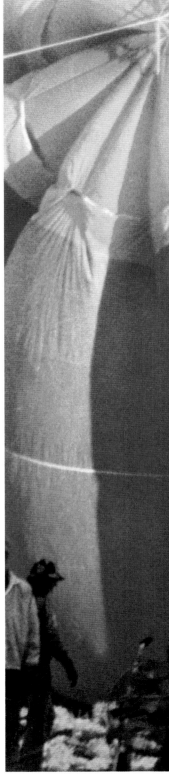

Barbara Van Cleve   *International Space Hall of Fame, Alamogordo (Top)*

Michael Rosenthal   *"Orpheus in the Underworld Descending," Santa Fe Opera (Above)*

Steven Northup   *Backstage, Santa Fe Festival Theater (Right)*

Barbara Erdman   *Balloon Fiesta, Albuquerque (Far Right)*

Carm Little Turtle *Desert Cowboy (hand colored sepia toned silver print)*

Jeannette Williams *Old Red Ball Cafe, Albuquerque*

Michael Heller *Shidoni Sculpture Garden, Tesuque*

Michael Heller *The Santa Fe police chasing a drunk driver*

Nicolas Secor *Gallery Opening, Santa Fe (Right)*

Murrae Haynes *Cocktail Party (Below)*

Murrae Haynes *"Not exactly Yehudi Menuhin" (Left)*

Nicolas Secor *Home Interior, Santa Fe (Below)*

Janet Russek   *Kitchen, Girls Group Home, Santa Fe*

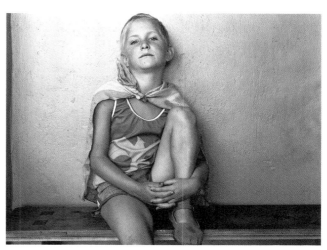

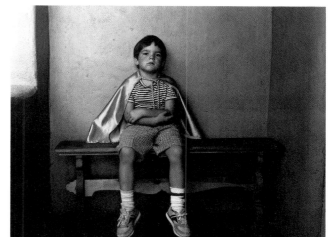

Janet Russek   *clockwise: Boomee, Devon, Laurel and Sky*

Helen Doroshow *Classroom, School for the Deaf, Santa Fe (Above Left)*

Helen Doroshow *School Bus (Above Right)*

Cissie Ludlow *Flag Day, Alto Street Day Care Center Santa Fe (Right)*

Edward Klamm *Graduation, Indian School, Paolo Soleri Theater, Santa Fe*

Mary Peck *House, New Mexico, from the New Mexico*
Photographic Survey, Museum of New Mexico,
funded by the National Endowment for the Arts
(Above)

Douglas Keats *Church Door, Dilia, N.M., 1984 (Right)*

Douglas Keats *Church, Anthony, N.M. 1984 (Far Right)*

Bernard Plossu   *Winter, Taos Pueblo*

William Davis *"Awaiting the Procession" Taos Pueblo, Christmas Eve*

David Scheinbaum *Children, Ranchos de las Golindrinas*
1980

Eliot Porter *Church, Velarde*

Nancy Hunter Warren *Blessing of the Fields Procession, San Ysidro*

Nancy Hunter Warren *Penitente 1*

Beaumont Newhall *Grave, Trampas, N.M. 1980*

Susan Steffy *"Nine Glories"*

Ray Belcher *"The White Door, Galisteo, 1982"*

Walter Chappell *The White Place near Abiquiu*

Stephen Cooper *South of Galisteo*

Ike Fordyce *Tent Rocks*

Lisa Law *Jemez Hot Springs*

David Noble *Route N.M. 57 near Chaco Canyon*

Robert Saltzman *Taos Graveyard*

Barbaraellen Koch *Rafting on the Rio Grande*

Herbert Lotz *Rio Grande Gorge, Taos*

Eliot Porter *White Sands*

Ray Belcher *Ruins, Galisteo*

Ray Belcher *Cemetery Galisteo*

THE PHOTOGRAPHERS

ROSWELL ANGIER

Mr. Angier's background includes employment as freelance photographer, lecturer, photographic editor of FUSION MAGAZINE (Boston) and photographic instructor. He is a recipient for the Visual Artists' Fellowship Award, National Endowment for the Arts. His works have been included in many publications, and are among the permanent collections of major museums in the United States, including the Fogg Museum, Boston. He is a graduate of Harvard University, 1962, and received two M.A. degrees from the University of California, Berkeley, 1964, 1965. Mr. Angier lives and works in Cambridge, Massachusetts. Pages 14, 35, 43, 64.

RAYMOND BELCHER

Born 1944, Mr. Belcher attended the San Francisco Art Institute. He has been actively involved in photography over the past two decades, and has an extensive history of group showings and juried exhibitions. He has had eight one man shows, most recently, "Selected Works 1964-1984" at the Santa Fe Center for Photography. His work appears in the book FACES AND FACADES, published by Polaroid. He is the recipient of the Photographer's Fellowship, National Endowment for the Arts, and has his photographs in numerous public and private collections. Mr. Belcher currently lives in Galisteo, New Mexico. Pages 96, 104, 105.

KEVIN BUBRISKI

Between 1975 and 1979, Mr. Bubriski lived in Nepal, where he photographed extensively. This work was later exhibited in New York and San Francisco. He studied at the Anthropological Film Center, Santa Fe, and has participated as still photographer, assistant cameraman, and director for several film productions. He has been awarded a grant by Harvard University to continue his Trans-Himalayan Photographic Survey, 1984-1987. His works are included in many public and private collections throughout the United States and have been published in numerous articles and magazines. His work appeared in POPULAR PHOTOGRAPHY's PHOTOGRAPHIC ANNUAL 1985. Pages 18, 20, 69.

PAUL CAPONIGRO

One of America's most renowned photographers, Mr. Caponigro was born in Boston, Massachusetts in 1932, studied photography with Minor White and began his notable career with his first one man show at the George Eastman House in 1958. His photographs are in all the major public collections in the United States. His books include THE WISE SILENCE and PAUL CAPONIGRO. His monographs include SUNFLOWERS and LANDSCAPE. While predominantly known for his large format photographs of the landscape (particularly rock formations such as Stonehenge in England) in black and white, Mr. Caponigro has fairly recently become interested in the 35mm format and is currently exploring color photography. Page 53.

WALTER CHAPPELL

Born 1925, Walter Chappell was a painter, craftsman, musician and poet living on the West Coast before discovering the art of photography in 1954. After working as assistant to Beaumont Newhall, George Eastman House, he became curator of exhibitions there between 1957 and 1961. His photographs are included in countless publications and are in the major museum collections through out the United States. He is also the recipient of three grants from the National Endowment for the Arts. His experimentations with high voltage, high frequency electronic impulses on fresh plants produced images of energy fields of those plants and resulted in his now famous portfolio METAFLORA. He was also the final editor for the film "Koyaanisqatsi." He lived in New Mexico between 1965 and 1970, and returned to the state in 1979, currently residing in Santa Fe. Pages 51, 97.

RAHOUL CONTRACTOR

Born 1953, Nesik, India, he began photographing at the age of thirteen. He continued his photographic studies at the San Francisco Art Institute, receiving his BFA degree in 1976. Mr. Contractor specializes in color technologies of photography. His works have been shown at the Art Institute, San Francisco and the Santa Fe Center for Photography, as well as in various galleries in India. Page 75.

STEPHEN COOPER

Stephen Cooper studied photography between 1964 and 1968 at the Educational Alliance, New York City. He received his M.F.A. degree in photography from the San Francisco Art Institute. Since 1965 his photographs have been included in over seventeen group exhibitions; he has also had three one man shows. Mr. Cooper currently lives in Albuquerque, New Mexico. Pages 45, 48, 98.

WILLIAM DAVIS
Mr. Davis lives and photographs in Taos, New Mexico. He is the founder/director of the DVS Gallery in Taos. His photographs have been included in many juried and invitational shows in Taos and Santa Fe. His work is the permanent collections of The Museum of Fine Arts, Santa Fe and the Harwood Museum, Taos. The PHOTOGRAPHERS' FORUM recently published an interview with him. Mr. Davis' photographs appear in the book IF MOUNTAINS DIE, published by Alfred Knopf. He continues to live and work in Taos. Pages 11, 52, 92.

ORLANDO DIAZ
Born 1953, Bogota, Colombia, South America, Mr. Diaz came to the United States to study at New York City College and Fort Lewis College. He became seriously involved with photography five years ago, and has since exhibited in galleries and public institutions in Santa Fe. He is currently working on personal projects. Page 73.

HELEN DOROSHOW
Born 1928, Philadelphia, she studied at the Art Institute of Chicago between 1966 and 1970. Her photographs have been included in numerous group exhibitions, and are included in private and public collections. She is the recipient of the Purchase Prize, New Mexico Museum of Fine Art, 1973. She is a member of the group documentation "A Portrait of Santa Fe 1983-1984", and a member of the project to document the Frank Lloyd Wright design known as the "Pottery House," Santa Fe. Ms. Doroshow lives in Santa Fe. Page 88.

BARBARA ERDMAN
Born in New York City, 1936, her background is that of a painter. She attended the Art Student's League, and received her B.F.A. degree from Cornell University in 1956. She lived in Italy intermittently from 1964 to 1977, based mainly in Firenze and Sesto Fiorentino. She started working in photography approximately five years ago. Her work has been included in numerous exhibitions and private collections. Her images have appeared in magazines including PHOTOGRAPHERS' FORUM BEST OF PHOTOGRAPHY, 1982 and she has recently published a color portfolio REFLECTIONS AND OTHER DIAGONALS. Ms. Erdman is currently the President of the Board of Directors, Santa Fe Center for Photography. She is the curator for "New Mexico, U.S.A.", and gained her knowledge of the area through her active political involvement with the feminist movement and particularly pro-choice activities. She is currently a resident of Santa Fe. Pages 7, 33, 42, 79.

RICHARD ERDOES
Born, 1912, in Frankfurt, Germany, he was brought up in Vienna, Austria. He studied at the Academy of Applied Art in Vienna, the Art Academy of Berlin, and the Academie de la Grande Chaumiere, Paris. He was a member of the anti-nazi underground. He moved to the United States in 1941. His photographs and illustrations have appeared in ATALANTE in Europe and in LIFE, THE SATURDAY EVENING POST, THE NEW YORK TIMES and HARPERS BAZAAR to mention only a few. He was awarded prizes by the New York Art Director's Club, the Society of Illustrators and The American Institute for Graphics Art. He began writing at the age of fifty and has now published more than a dozen books, fiction and non-fiction. He has created and published photographic books on Ireland, Ancient Rome, and the Sioux, Pueblo and Navajo Indians. Mr. Erdoes has been an activist in the Native American civil rights movement and was given an Indian name by seven medicine men in a Sioux ceremonial. Mr. Erdoes lives in New York City and Santa Fe. Pages 21, 23, 24, 29.

MICHAEL FAHY
Mr. Fahy is a commercial photographer who works in both black and white and color formats. He is the recipient of awards in the Professional Division, 1981, New Mexico State Fair, in color and black and white categories. Employed as a geological engineer, he uses the opportunity to photograph the landscape in the remote parts of New Mexico that most people never see. He lives in Albuquerque. Page 75.

IKE FORDYCE
Born and raised in the ranching country of northern Wyoming, Mr. Fordyce is a relative newcomer to New Mexico and to photography. He became seriously involved with the medium in 1980 after moving to Santa Fe from his ranch in Wyoming. His images are, for most part, concerned with the aesthetics of the land forms found in the western mountain ranges. He has begun showing his works in New Mexico and the other Rocky Mountain States. He is represented by Scheinbaum & Russek gallery in Santa Fe. Pages 9, 99.

BARBARA GLUCK
After a ten year career as a New York advertising art director, Barbara Gluck became a photographer in South Vietnam in 1968, just after the TET offensive. Her first assignments were for the Associated Press and TIME magazine. She spent three and a half years covering the war for THE NEW YORK TIMES and NEWSWEEK. She was the first woman to fly a B52 mission and spend time with the Vietcong. She moved to Santa Fe in 1976 and has continued to work for national magazines and newspapers on assignments throughout the west. Her fine arts photography has been shown in museums, galleries and universities throughout the United States. In 1983 Ms. Gluck conceived the project "Portrait of Santa Fe 1983-1984, A Point of Balance", a project in which 14 photographers and two writers documented the city for one year. An exhibit of the work opened at the Palace of the Governors in Santa Fe in the summer of 1985. Ms. Gluck is currently working on a new project called "The Universe Within My Crystal Ball." Pages 38, 67.

DON GREISER
Born in Indiana in 1955, Mr. Greiser studied photography at Indiana University with Henry Holmes Smith. He received his degree in 1978. His approaches to photographic imagery include multi-exposure panoramic strips, night photography, and hand-colored photographs. His works are included in the collections of the Center for Creative Photography, Tucson and the Indiana University Art Museum. He has exhibited throughout the mid and southwest, most recently in "Southwest '85", Museum of Fine Arts, Santa Fe. For the past six years he has lived in Pine Hill, New Mexico, working for the Ramah Navajo School Board as the production manager for the Tsa' Azzi' Graphics Center. He is a member of the Gallup Area Arts Council. Page 65.

JAMES HART
Born in 1952, in Portland, Oregon, Mr. Hart received his M.F.A. degree in Photographic Studies from the Visual Studies Workshop at SUNY, Buffalo, New York. He is the former coordinator of traveling exhibitions, Visual Studies Workshop, and Coordinator of the Photographic Programs for the Gates-Chili Public Schools, New York. Mr. Hart currently lives in Santa Fe, and is a member of the team working on "Portrait of Santa Fe, 1983-1984". He is a freelance photographer. Pages 17, 19, 39.

MURRAE HAYNES
Mr. Haynes is a photo journalist and commercial photographer living in Santa Fe. He is currently photo editor for THE SANTA FE REPORTER, a weekly newspaper, and a freelance photographer for United Press International. He is part owner of the Santa Fe Photo District, a photographic studio used for the production of commercial still-life and fashion photography. Pages 38, 84, 85, Front Cover.

MICHAEL HELLER
Born 1946, he studied at New York University and the University of California, majoring in photography. Mr. Heller is a photojournalist who has worked with THE EVENING OUTLOOK in Santa Monica, California, and the ALBUQUERQUE JOURNAL, New Mexico. He is currently photography editor for THE NEW MEXICAN in Santa Fe. His photographs have received awards from the National Press Photographer's Assn., Associated Press and the New Mexico Press Assn. His photographs have been published in TIME, POPULAR PHOTOGRAPHY, AMERICAN PHOTOGRAPHER, THE NEW YORK TIMES, and TIME-LIFE BOOKS, to mention a few. Mr. Heller is a resident of Santa Fe. Pages 82, 83.

BRADNER CRAWFORD JONES
Mr. Jones is a fourth generation New Mexican, born in 1944. He received his B.A. degree in geology from New Mexico Highlands University and a degree in electronics from the Cleveland School of Electronics. He began his interest in photography in 1977, and continued with further study at the School of Modern Photography. His work has been included in several publications and group exhibitions. He maintains his photographic interests as a professional and fine art photographer. Mr. Jones has lived in Santa Fe since 1974, and is employed by the railroad. Pages 46, 47.

DOUGLAS KAHN
Born in 1940, Mr. Kahn studied at the New York University School of Engineering and then continued his studies at Pratt Institute, receiving his degree in architecture, 1967. He was an architect in the firms of Marcel Breuer, and later with Richard Meier. Eventually, he opened his own architectural firm. In 1980 he transferred his interests to architectural and fine arts photography. He has travelled extensively in Asia, the Middle East and Europe. His work as an architect has been published in DOMUS, and in the French and British editions of HOUSE AND GARDEN MAGAZINE. His work as a photographer has been published in ABITARE. He has participated in numerous group shows in the Southwest and makes his home in Santa Fe. Pages 49, 58.

DOUGLAS KEATS
Born in 1948, Mr. Keats grew up in Texas. He received his B.A. degree in 1977 from Washington and Lee University. He is a self-taught photographer who works primarily with a large format view camera. He is noted for his images of the female nude and recently he has begun amassing a large body of work on the old Spanish churches throughout New Mexico. His works are included in several public collections including the Museum of Fine Arts, Houston, Texas. He is represented by Ernesto Mayans Gallery in Santa Fe. Page 90.

EDWARD KLAMM
Mr. Klamm is a well known freelance photojournalist whose work has been published by NEWSWEEK, TIME and United Press International. His assignments have included working for U.S. NEWS AND WORLD REPORT, AMERICAN PHOTOGRAPHER, NBC NEWS, and the LONDON ECONOMIST. He is director of the Fotowest Picture Agency, Santa Fe, and project director of the year long documentation of Santa Fe: "Portrait of Santa Fe, 1983-1984." He is publisher of the book SANTA FE, CITY IN PHOTOGRAPHS. DUSTOFF, a book of his photographs was published by the Institute of American Indian Arts Press. He has twice been the winner of the E.H. Shaffer Award, and is represented by Blackstar, New York. Mr. Klamm lives in Santa Fe. Pages 34, 40, 89.

ROBERT KLINTWORTH
Mr. Klintworth's visual interests include filmmaking, television production, painting, sculpture as well as photography. His films have received awards from the American Film Festival and the North Carolina Film Festival. His photographs have appeared in numerous publications including THE NEW YORK TIMES. Mr. Klintworth lives in Santa Fe. Page 44.

BARBARAELLEN KOCH
Born 1951, Ms. Koch studied at the University of New York, New Palz and at the University of Maine. She began her photojournalism career in 1974 with the MAINE FREE WOMEN'S HERALD. After moving to Santa Fe, she worked with THE SANTA FE REPORTER, and THE NEW MEXICAN newspaper where she became chief photographer. Currently she is chief photographer for THE ALBUQUERQUE JOURNAL NORTH, and staff photographer for the ALBUQUERQUE JOURNAL. Her photographs have received awards from the National Press Photographers Assn., and have been published in LIFE magazine, AMERICAN PHOTOGRAPHER and the French publication ACTUEL. Ms. Koch makes her home in Santa Fe. Pages 41, 44, 66, 102.

LISA LAW
Since 1962 Lisa Law has been documenting the social changes in the United States by photographing the Rock and Roll musicians of the West Coast, the "flower children" of San Francisco, the anti-war demonstrations and the migrations of the hippies to New Mexico. She continues today to document musicians and their involvement in the peace movement. She is also staff photographer for the Telluride and Santa Fe Film Festivals, and for the Santa Fe Festival Theatre. Her commercial work includes album covers, portraits, magazine articles and photographs for publicity and advertising. She has had three one-person exhibitions, and has shown in over ten group shows. Her works have appeared in eleven publications and she is presently preparing a book for publication on the '60's. Her home is in Santa Fe. Pages 13, 46, 47, 99.

J. D. LINCOLN
J. D. Lincoln, born in Cambridge, Massachusetts, is known primarily for his photographs of people and began camera work at the age of nine. He has appeared in many exhibitions in New England and New York, and has published the book PEOPLE OF PORTSMOUTH. He currently resides in Santa Fe, where he works as a still photographer and video producer. Page 62.

CARM LITTLE TURTLE
Born in California in 1952, Carm Little Turtle is a Mescalero Apache Indian. She studied at the Santa Barbara Community Art College, and continued her studies at the Navajo Community College, Arizona where she received degrees in nursing and art. Her work is in museum collections throughout the West. Her photographs are sepia toned and then hand colored. She works and lives in Taos, N.M. Pages 27, 80.

PAUL LOGSDON
Pilot-photographer Paul Logsdon uses his home in Santa Fe as a base for his aerial photography of the Southwest. Using a hand-held camera, he creates images that reveal unique perspectives of the natural and man-made landscapes. His photographs are included in several museum collections, the most notable being the Metropolitan Museum of Art in New York. His images have been published by the British Broadcasting Co., TIME-LIFE and the NATIONAL GEOGRAPHIC magazine. His works are to be shown in the two major survey exhibitions opening in Santa Fe the summer of 1985, "Survey of New Mexico, 1982" and "Portrait of Santa Fe, 1983-1984". His color and black and white prints are in several corporate and private collections. Pages 30, 31.

HERB LOTZ
Born 1944, Mr. Lotz studied at the University of Chicago and the Art Institute of Chicago in a special joint program with dual majors in design and photography. He continued his studies in photography at the University of New Mexico's graduate seminar program. Mr. Lotz is an established commercial photographer, as well as a fine arts photographer. His work has appeared in many exhibitions in New Mexico, Texas, California and Kansas. He lives and works in Santa Fe. Page 102.

CISSIE LUDLOW
Born 1945, she received her B.F.A. degree in painting from the Maryland Institute College of Art. After working as Assistant to the Designer for Installations, Baltimore Museum of Art, she lived in London for several years. She began photographing in 1976, studied at the Maine Photo Workshop, 1979, and was employed by the Center for Creative Photography 1980-1981, cataloging the archive of photographer Wynn Bullock. She is the former coordinator of exhibitions at the Santa Fe Center for Photography. Her photographs are in public and private collections, and have been in numerous group exhibitions. She is a participant in Live Video Theatre, Santa Fe. She is represented by the Scheinbaum & Russek Gallery of Photography in Santa Fe. Ms. Ludlow has lived in Santa Fe since 1972. Pages 70, 71, 88.

JUDY ELLEN MOORE
Born 1941, in Philadelphia, she attended the Rhode Island School of Design and Cornell University, where she received her B.F.A. degree in 1963. She became a serious student of photography under the instruction of Don Erceg, a Minor White disciple. After moving to California, she studied photography at San Francisco State University, exploring the possibilities of composing and photographing arranged imagery, and developing her skills as a color printer. She moved to New Mexico in 1984 and continues her studies in art history and photography at the University of New Mexico. Page 26.

BEAUMONT NEWHALL
Born 1908, Lynn, Massachusetts, Beaumont Newhall is the world's foremost photographic historian. He studied art history under the noted Dr. Paul Sachs at Harvard University, where he received both his B.A. and M.A. degrees. He has worked for the Philadelphia Museum of Art, the Metropolitan Museum, and the Museum of Modern Art, New York. He was the major factor in the development of the two major art centers for photographic study in the United States, the Museum of Modern Art in New York City and the George Eastman House, Rochester, New York. After moving to New Mexico, he established the first graduate school of photography in the country at the University of New Mexico. His book, THE HISTORY OF PHOTOGRAPHY, has been printed in five languages. He is the recipient of countless awards and medals in photography. During his distinguished career as historian, writer and curator, Dr. Newhall was also making his own photographs, which have only recently been exhibited. His portraits included photographers who have become legends. His still-lifes reflect his direct and spontaneous approach of the 35mm camera. In 1983 his first book of photographs IN PLAIN SIGHT was published by Gibbs M. Smith, Peregrine Smith Books. Because of his writing, teaching and research, New Mexico has become one of the country's leading photographic centers. Dr. Newhall is represented by the Scheinbaum & Russek Gallery of Photography in Santa Fe. Page 95.

DAVID GRANT NOBLE
Born 1939, Boston, Massachusetts, Mr. Noble received his B.A. degree from Yale University. A self-taught photographer, his interest in the medium began during his tenure with the U.S. Army, 1961-1964. After moving to Santa Fe in 1972, he became a member of the staff of the School of American Research. He has had ten one-person shows, and has participated in twice that number of group exhibitions seen throughout the United States. His photographs have appeared in numerous publications, and are included in public and private collections. His books include ANCIENT RUINS OF THE SOUTHWEST, Northland Press, 1981, now in its fifth printing, and NEW LIGHT ON CHACO CANYON, School of American Research Press, 1984. His photographs are represented by the Scheinbaum & Russek Gallery of Photography, Santa Fe. Pages 10, 11, 22, 100.

STEVE NORTHUP
Steve Northup grew up in Santa Fe and was educated in the public school system, graduating from Santa Fe High School in 1959. He began his career in photography with the SANTA FE NEW MEXICAN, a daily newspaper, while in Junior High School. He has been a staff photographer with the United Press International at the San Francisco, Miami and Saigon Bureaus. In 1967, he joined the WASHINGTON POST newspaper and in 1972 became a photographer for TIME magazine in the Washington, D.C. Bureau. In 1973-74 he was a Nieman Fellow at Harvard University and in 1984 was on the Nieman selection committee. His home is in Santa Fe. Pages 32, 78.

JACK PARSONS
After receiving his B.A. and M.A. degrees from the University of Colorado, Mr. Parsons went on to study film at the London School of Film Technique, in England. His visual and creative interests have continued to embrace cinematography, still photography, and writing. He has produced and photographed over twenty films, and his still photographs have been included in numerous publications and books, including SANTA FE, THE CITY IN PHOTOGRAPHS, published by FotoWest, and COWBOY, written by Russell Martin. He is Vice-President and Treasurer, Public Media, Inc. of Santa Fe, and a partner in Blue Sky Productions, Santa Fe. He photographs in both black and white and color. His still photographs have been in numerous exhibitions throughout the Southwest, and are included in the permanent collection of the Museum of Fine Art, Santa Fe. Pages 12, 61, 74.

MARY PECK
Born in 1952, in Minneapolis, she apprenticed to Paul Caponigro and to the late Laura Gilpin. She is co-founder of the Santa Fe Center for Photography, and curated the most popular exhibition shown there, "Santa Fe: Past and Present." Her photographs have been exhibited nationally, and her works are included in many public and private collections throughout the United States. She is a member of the group documentation "The New Mexico Survey, 1983," sponsored by the New Mexico Museum of Fine Arts, Santa Fe. She is noted for her portfolio of photographs TEMPLES OF GREECE. Her home is in Santa Fe. Pages 55, 57, 90.

DEEDE PHILLIPS
Born in 1922, New York City, Ms. Phillips is a self-taught photographer whose interest in the medium began in 1979. After moving to Santa Fe in 1980, she has continued to pursue her photographic interests. She is currently producing a color documentation of an isolated area in Northern New Mexico. Pages 25, 72.

BERNARD PLOSSU
Born 1945, in Viet Nam of French parents, Mr. Plossu has lived in New Mexico since 1977. His photographs have been exhibited internationally, and are included in public and pri-

vate collections throughout Europe and the United States. His books include NEW MEXICO REVISITED, 1983, EGYPTE, 1979, LE VOYAGE MEXICAIN, 1979 and SURBANALISM, 1972. He is represented by the Ernesto Mayans Gallery, Santa Fe. He photographs exclusively with a 35mm camera and works in both black and white and color. Pages 59, 60, 91.

ELIOT PORTER
Born in Winnetka, Illinois in 1901. Eliot Porter has been a resident of Santa Fe since 1946. A graduate of the Harvard Medical School, he began photographing as an avocation. After his one-man show at Alfred Stieglitz's An American Place, in 1929, he made photography his life's work. Considered to be the unchallenged master of color photography, his dye transfer prints reflect the beauty of nature and wild-life. One of the most respected contemporary masters of photography, Porter's wide ranging travels to every corner of the globe are recorded in an extensive body of work. His sensitivity to the natural landscape and an unparalleled technical ability have earned him an important position in the annals of photography. In 1979-80 Mr. Porter was honored by the first one-man exhibit of color photographs ever presented at the Metropolitan Museum of Art in New York. He has published numerous books and portfolios including, INTIMATE LANDSCAPES, ANTARCTICA, both published by Dutton, ICELAND and ALL UNDER HEAVEN, his book on China. His is represented by the Scheinbaum and Russek Gallery, Santa Fe. Pages 93, 103.

MICHAEL ROSENTHAL
Mr. Rosenthal is the staff photographer for the Santa Fe Opera. His photographs have appeared in national publications, including TIME magazine. Page 78.

MERIDEL RUBENSTEIN
Born 1948, Ms. Rubenstein received her M.A. and M.F.A. degrees from the University of New Mexico. Her background includes many years of teaching photography in university and workshop programs. Her photographs have been exhibited worldwide including Mexico City, Arles and Paris as well as throughout the United States. Her book LA GENTE DE LA LUZ was published in 1977. The prints were shown in Germany. She is noted for the range of processes that she has mastered including palladium, platinum, and color. She is a participant in the "New Mexico Survey, 1983", sponsored by

the Museum of Fine Arts, Santa Fe. Ms. Rubenstein was a recipient of a Guggenheim Fellowship in 1981-82 and of the Photographer's Fellowship from the National Endowment for the Arts in 1983. She is living in Santa Fe. Page 13.

JAMES DAVID RUFFNER
Born 1942, Rochester, New York, Mr. Ruffner is the owner/director of the Photogenesis Gallery and Workshop in Albuquerque, New Mexico. His background includes many years of teaching photography at all levels. He was the assistant curator of photography at the Jacksonville Art Museum, Jacksonville, Florida. He received an M.F.A. degree in photography from the Visual Studies Workshop, Rochester, New York. He has had numerous one-man exhibitions throughout the United States. Pages 15, 56.

JANET RUSSEK
Born in 1947, Brooklyn, New York, Ms. Russek received her B.A. degree from Hunter College, and her M.A. degree from Brooklyn College in 1973. She studied conservation and preservation of works on paper at the Brooklyn Museum where she was employed until her move to Santa Fe in 1980. She is the co-owner and director of the Scheinbaum & Russek Gallery of Photography in Santa Fe. Ms. Russek assists Eliot Porter in the cataloging and conservation of his print collection. Her photographs have been included in several group shows and traveling exhibitions, and her work was recently published in CREATIVE CAMERA, London, 1984. Pages 17, 86, 87.

ROBERT SALTZMAN
Born in 1945, Mr. Saltzman began photographing after years as a working musician. His photographic imagery explores his interest in the sexuality found in the forms of the landscape as well as the human body. His photographs have been shown in several major exhibitions, and are in the collections of public and private archives. Mr. Saltzman is a resident of Taos, New Mexico. Pages 54, 101.

DAVID SCHEINBAUM
Born in Brooklyn, New York, 1951, Mr. Scheinbaum began teaching photography in 1974 at Pace University, New York City. He continued teaching until his move to Santa Fe in 1978. At that time, he became assistant to the notable photographic historian, Beaumont Newhall. Mr. Scheinbaum is a master printer, who prints in black and white for both Beaumont Newhall and Eliot Porter. He is instructor of photography at the College of Santa Fe, and co-owner and director of the

Scheinbaum & Russek Gallery of Photography, Santa Fe. His photo essays include MIAMI and JASON: A HOMEBIRTH EXPERIENCE. He is currently completing a landscape project on the Bisti Badlands, an endangered area of New Mexico. BISTI is scheduled to be published by the University of New Mexico Press in 1986. His photographs have appeared in many shows throughout the United States and are part of the permanent collections of numerous museums and universities in the United States and Europe. Pages 16, 50, 93.

NICHOLAS SECOR
Mr. Secor lives in Santa Fe, and is in co-partnership with Murrae Haynes operating Northstar Productions. He is completing his book A PHOTOGRAPHIC ESSAY OF THE UNITED STATES MARINE CORPS, which will be published by the summer of 1986. He is a member of the Santa Fe Photo District Studio, and freelances in commercial and photo journalism. He is employed by THE SANTA FE REPORTER, a weekly newspaper. Pages 84, 85.

BARBARA SIMPSON
Born 1950 in New Jersey, she began her studies in photography at the University of New Mexico where she received her B.A. degree in Fine Arts. She has been actively involved in the medium for the past five years. Most representative of her creative interest in photography are her large hand-painted prints that reflect the varied and changing cultures in the state of New Mexico. She has been a Santa Fe resident for the past ten years. Pages 28, 76.

SUSAN STEFFY
Born in 1945 in North Carolina, Ms. Steffy received her B.A. degree in genetics from the University of California, Berkeley. Her photographs have been included in numerous invitational and group exhibitions in the United States. Her black and white portfolio, FIVE INSIDE was produced in 1982, and her work is also included in the group portfolio PORTFOLIO 1 produced by the Santa Fe Center for Photography. She is currently living in Galisteo, New Mexico. Page 96.

ALEX TRAUBE
Born in 1946, New York City, he received his M.A. degree in photography from Ohio University in 1970 and also studied privately with Minor White. In 1976 he received the National Endowment for the Arts Fellowship. His photographs have been included in many group exhibitions and are also among the collections of private and corporate investors. He published his book LAS VEGAS, NEW MEXICO: A PORTRAIT, 1984, and is currently teaching photography at the Santa Fe Preparatory School. Pages 38, 65, 68.

BARBARA VAN CLEVE
Born in ranching country, Montana in 1935, Ms. Van Cleve received her M.A. degree from Northwestern University and later studied photography at Columbia College, Chicago. She was a college professor for over twenty years before devoting herself full-time to her commercial and fine art photography. She has shown her photographs throughout the country, and has her work in the permanent collections of the Museum of Fine Arts, Santa Fe, as well as in numerous publications. Recently she produced A FRESH LOOK AT THE RODEO COW-BOY, a 1986 calendar. She is represented by the Andrew Smith Gallery, Albuquerque, and Images West in Santa Fe. She resides mainly in Santa Fe, but returns every year to Montana to work on the family ranch. Pages 28, 63, 78.

WILLARD VAN DYKE
Born 1906, Denver, Colorado Willard Van Dyke began his photographic career with his apprenticeship to Edward Weston in 1929. Three years later, he was co-founder of the now famous group, F-64. In the following years he turned his creative energies to filmmaking, which he continued to produce, direct and photograph until 1968. In 1965 he was appointed Director of the Department of Film, Museum of Modern Art in New York, and in 1973 he left MOMA to establish the film department at the State University of New York. His photographs are included in over twenty museum collections. He recently moved to Santa Fe where he continues to photograph, write and teach. Page 52.

CHARLES VENRICK
Born 1914, Crete, Nebraska, he received his B.A. degree from Dartmouth College in 1936. Between 1936 and 1951 he was employed by the American Locomotive Co., and by ACF Industries Inc. He became seriously interested in photography in 1968, and has since participated in numerous exhibitions throughout New Mexico. He is one of the co-founders of the Santa Fe Center for Photography and past President of its Board of Directors. Pages 37, 77.

NANCY HUNTER WARREN
Born in Buffalo, New York, she studied at the University of Delaware. She is a self-taught photographer, whose photographs have been included in numerous publications and exhibitions. She has been on the staff of the Museum of New Mexico, Laboratory of Anthropology since 1974, and is the photographer for the Spanish Colonial Arts Society. Ms. Warren has been published in various magazines and anthropological bulletins. She lives in Santa Fe. Pages 36, 69, 94, 95.

JOHN WHATLEY
Born in 1947, Mr. Whatley received his university degree in applied science and management. He is the owner of a color processing lab in Santa Fe. His photographs of Carlsbad Caverns were taken in available light using high-speed film. Page 72.

RICHARD WICKSTROM
Born in 1946, in Chicago, Mr. Wickstrom received his M.A. and his M.F.A. degrees from the University of Iowa, in art history and photography. He has been the Associate Curator of Prints and Photography at the University of Iowa, Museum of Art, and the Director, Senior Curator, University Art Gallery, New Mexico State University. He was the Director of the C.J. Rein Gallery, Santa Fe in 1983, and also a past President of the Board of Directors of the Santa Fe Center for Photography. After moving to Santa Fe he founded Lightworks of Santa Fe, Inc., which specializes in color printing. Mr. Wickstrom works in both black and white and color photography and is considered a master color printer. Pages 27, 57.

JEANNETTE WILLIAMS
Jeannette Williams moved to New Mexico in 1963 from California. She received a B.A. in Design from San Jose State University and an M.A. from the University of New Mexico. As a photographer, she is primarily self-taught. Her main interest is in photographing people. She began showing her photographs in 1974 and has been in many group and invitational shows in Taos, Santa Fe, and Albuquerque as well as Texas and Colorado. She has traveled extensively in Europe, Central America, and Mexico. Recently, she had two one woman shows of her photographs from Kenya at the Santa Fe Center for Photography and The Ruth Ramberg gallery in Albuquerque. She has been published in NEW MEXICO, A GUIDE TO THE STATE and THE BEST OF PHOTOGRAPHY ANNUAL, 1982, 1983 and 1984 put out by PHOTOGRAPHER'S FORUM MAGAZINE. Pages 35, 56, 66, 81.

SUSAN ZWINGER
Ms. Zwinger is a staff member of the Fine Arts Museum of New Mexico, in Santa Fe. She began photographing while she was employed with THE SANTA FE REPORTER, a weekly newspaper, as photo critic. Her other artistic interests include painting and writing. Page 25.

MARY SHAPIRO
Mary Shapiro designed this catalogue. She studied design at State University College of Buffalo, N.Y., and the University of Copenhagen, Denmark. She received her B.F.A. degree from Parsons School of Design in New York City. Ms. Shapiro has been a graphic designer with Chanticleer Press, and has worked together with the Will Hopkins Group, and Vignelli Associates. She was a graphic designer for CONNOISSEUR Magazine and numerous computer publications at Ziff-Davis Publishing Company. She is presently a freelance designer for NEW MEXICO MAGAZINE and is living in Santa Fe.